The Stranger in the Polka Dot Tie

How I Found My Father

The Stranger in the Polka Dot Tie

How I Found My Father

Sandra Lee Cleary

FRANKLIN
SCRIBES™
PUBLISHERS

Copyright © 2019 by Sandra Lee Cleary

All rights reserved. No part of this book may be used or reproduced in any manner whatsoever without the written permission of the author.

Cleary, Sandra Lee

The Stranger in the Polka Dot Tie:
How I Found My Father

First Edition
Reference: Genealogy

Library of Congress Control Number: 2019900921

ISBN Paperback: 978-1-941516-47-8
ISBN eBook: 978-1-941516-48-5

Large Print Edition in 15 pt. Oldstyle

Published by Franklin Scribes Publishers. Franklin Scribes is a registered trademark of Franklin Scribes Publishers.

franklinscribeswrites@gmail.com
franklinscribes.com

Contact the author at
franklinscribes.com/sandra-lee-cleary/
journeythroughourbranches.com/

Editor: Judy Sheer Watters

This book was printed in the United States of America.

Dedication

This is for you, Mom, and the secret you lived with all your life. I'm so sorry you felt like you couldn't confide in me. I often wonder what you were thinking when you looked at me. Were you looking for a resemblance to my father? Or, were the words right there on the tip of your tongue never making their way out of your mouth. Oh, how you must have hurt at times wanting to tell me, but the timing wasn't right, or you didn't know how to express the things that happened so long ago. You did a good job raising my siblings and me, and you should have no regrets. You were a strong woman doing for your family the best you could following your upbringing ways handed down to you. I love you, Mom, and always will. You did well.

Life is a Puzzle

As a young child of ten, I watched my parents open the puzzle box and dump the pieces out on the card table set up in our living room. I even helped turn over all the pieces, so they could begin piecing the frame around the picture. Occasionally, I, too, found a snippet and placed it in its correct space helping to bring the picture to fruition.

Mesmerized, I watched them lay each craggy piece into the picture. It seemed like in no time the puzzle was finished, then they'd start another one to while away their time at night. We only had a radio to listen to. That was before television, but after the dark ages.

Fast forward seventy years and I have watched my life unfold like that of a puzzle. Each segment has finally been placed in its specific place revealing the story of my emergence. It began with small barbs at age four from my grandmother, like when I pointed to a picture of my father and she quickly said, "No he isn't, and don't ever call him your father." Not knowing what she was talking about, I soon forgot what was said and went about my business.

When I was fifteen, Dad, who was in the Army, was being shipped to Germany; so, Mom and Dad took a trip to Minnesota to visit family before he had to leave. Grandma was left in charge of my siblings and me. My boyfriend called and asked me to go for a ride and get a coke. I asked grandma if I could go. She grabbed the phone and hung up then began yelling at me. "You're no good. You are just like your mother. You'll never amount to anything."

Stunned, I screamed back at her. "Why are you saying that? There's nothing wrong with my mother." I began to cry. My stomach knotted. What was grandma talking about? I headed for the door to breathe in some fresh air. Grandma was right on my heels pulling my shirt tail. I wrenched myself free and bolted but not before all my buttons popped off. I grabbed my shirt together and ran for my neighbor's house next door, grandma still shrieking.

Upon Mom's return I told her what had transpired. "Mom, what was Grandma talking about? Why would she say those things about you?"

She replied, "I'll have a talk with her. I don't know what she was talking about. I wouldn't worry about it."

A few years passed, but I had a gnawing feeling growing inside me I couldn't shake. Sometimes when Mom and I were alone I'd ask her again about the things Grandma had said. She brushed my question off by saying, "She won't be watching you kids anymore." Then she would turn and walk away from me. I began to think there was more to what Grandma had said but I couldn't put my finger on anything specific. More years went by.

I didn't finally come to terms with how I felt about the oppressive feeling hidden deep within until I was in my twenties. I wanted to know more about my past and why my mother told me my father wasn't my father when I was eight years old. Out of the blue, as my siblings and I were playing, she announced, "He is not your father." Stunned, I asked her, "If he isn't my father, then who is?" There was no answer.

All my life up into my twenties that was my mother's answer – silence. Just once she gave me his name, then nothing. I asked to see my birth certificate. She said, "The Army needed it to prove you lived under your stepfather's roof. I sent it to them, and they never returned it." That was why I used my step-father's name. End of story.

In 1969 my children attended a four-room native-rock school for the last year as the school was finally closing. They would begin classes in the new school, which sat higher up the mountain in Devore, California. I was asked to do research on the old school originally built in the early 1900's as a one-room school. The new school wanted the information to put into a time capsule. I enjoyed doing the research so much. I realized then that I could probe records and find information on my biological father.

In 1969 I sent my first letter, hand written, to the Department of Army asking if they had an address for my father as I was trying to get in touch with him. This dispatch was long before computers. It was a long shot but worth a try. It took only two months to get the answer and with his last known address. Thank you, Jesus.

Another two months passed before I found the courage to write. Time dragged on, or so it felt. Finally, after four months, I received an answer from him. He told me he was a mechanic, had a home in Minnesota which he'd been working on, he was remarried, and he had a son who just finished high school. He never acknowledged me, never said I was his daughter, nothing to that effect. I was hurt, didn't know what to think, but folded the letter and placed it back in the envelope. Later, I put the letter in a small box, along with all my other papers I needed to keep. End of story.

Confused and perplexed, I tried pushing my feelings deep down into the recesses of my being. If I didn't think or allow my feelings to show, no one would know how I felt. Still, why didn't he admit I was his daughter?

I didn't follow up on searching for answers for quite some time. Raising children, moving, and life took precedence. Not until

Mom's passing in 1995 did I honestly start researching my family tree. Ancestry, heritage, a family's legacy was beginning to surface in magazines and on television. I joined the band wagon.

I started writing letters, tons of letters, to complete strangers and praying they would answer me and my questions. Little by little, one small question after another.

With my first computer bought in 1995, I began searching every ancestry site I could find. I bought a white board and set it opposite my desk. Then, I started adding names. I wanted to see how each person was related and how they connected to me.

My final quest was DNA. All of this put together led me to the realization that my mother went to great lengths to hide her indiscretion as a young woman. Although I found out what happened to my mother, being angry would be of no benefit to anyone. I can truthfully feel compassion for her and what she endured throughout her life.

So many times, I asked her about my father and her answer was always the same:

"He was a nice man. I suppose he still lives in Minnesota." Her standard answer, nothing more, nothing less.

When I visited my mother, we would sit together in the evening and watch television, have a drink, and talk. Surface talk, nothing deep, no questions answered. Oh, how I wish I had known the right question to ask to get the answers I was searching for. I guess that was her way of coping.

I don't love her any less for it. I've asked myself if I were my mother, would I have the courage to talk about my life to my children. It was a different time for her. A time when you didn't talk about your life, loves, or family. You kept things to yourself. And, after all, there was a war going on. Her life was in an upheaval with her husband gone to fight half way around the world. A place she only read about in books or heard about on the radio.

Well, Mom, I'm going to tell your story. I pray when people read this, they will understand you better and rejoice in my finding my biological father.

I also hope that in telling my story to

find my biological dad, you, dear reader, will be encouraged to find the answers to your pressing questions.

Lions and Tigers and Bears, oh My!

A year after Mom's passing in 1995, my husband and I took a trip to Washington to visit my younger brother, Danny. My brother, Chuck, met us at Danny's for a reunion. I was going through some of mom's photo albums and started pointing out people. Of course, she had written dates and names under most of the pictures which made it easier.

Dan said, "How do you know all these people?"

"Mom talked about these people in the photos. That's the only reason I know."

"Well, why don't you take all the picture albums home with you," he offered.

"Danny, they are your relatives too. Why should I take them?"

"You're the oldest, and besides, after you figure out the "who" and the "what" about the people, you can make copies for the rest of us. Go on, pack them in your suitcase and take them with you."

"Well, Mom left the albums with you. If you're sure you don't mind, I'll take them."

"No problem, Sis. I don't mind. Besides, maybe you can figure out some strange mystery from the pictures," he said laughing.

Little did he know then what kind of a mystery began to unfold. Danny would not live long enough to hear all the story. Both Danny and his wife passed away from cancer within two years of each other, Danny in 2007 and his wife, Gail, in 2009.

At Danny's urging, I took as many of the albums as I could pack away in my suitcase for my trip home from Oklahoma. Thus, began my intense journey into my mother's past. Oh, what a tangled web we weave when first we practice to deceive. My mother's life and mine took so many twists and turns.

At first, I sat for hours looking through the albums. Staring at each picture trying to remember what Mom had said about the person. I was overjoyed she dated one album along with putting the person's name under each picture. One album, on the front-page, she wrote *Album of Mrs. Annabell Eisentrager 1941*. The year before I was born. All this information made it easier when I tried putting a timeline together.

I found a newspaper clipping of her best friend, Ruth, when she married Hugo. There were pictures of Alan and Mom embracing. Alan's last name was the same as Ruth's, so I figured they were brother and sister. This was later corroborated when I wrote a letter to Ruth asking questions about my mother. However, when I received a reply it was from Ruth's husband, Hugo. He explained Ruth had passed away a couple of years earlier, and all he could tell me was Alan and Mom were sweet on each other. I wondered if maybe they had an affair, then went their separate ways.

Another picture caught my attention. From the date below the picture, I knew she was married at the time, but she was holding hands with someone other than her husband. Her head laid on his shoulder, and clearly, you could tell she was happy. I thought he may have been a relative.

Still on another page held a picture of her husband in uniform standing on the front porch with about a foot of snow covering the ground dated Jan 1941. Caption said *Roy*, the man she was married to.

Then I came across one more picture of a man in uniform, standing in front of a car, and underneath it said, *Soldier boy from Waterloo*. Next to that picture was one of the same man, but this time, the caption said *Junior Waverly*.

The set of pictures that really caught my eye were the ones where Grandma, Mom, and Junior were standing alongside the road, Junior in uniform, and a couple of Civilian Conservation Corp (CCC) boys. Mom and Junior held hands and looked quite friendly. Then another picture of Mom and Junior standing in front of Buffalo Bill Cody's grave in Golden, Colorado puzzled me. I'd never heard anything about this.

Along with Mom's albums were several of her mother's. A couple of Grandma's albums had names and dates. She also had pictures of Junior Waverly. Well now, he must be a relative, but I didn't remember anyone talking about him.

I found wedding pictures of Mom and Roy with Grandma standing with them. I could go on and on about pictures and who the captions said they were, but the ones that were important I've named.

I stored the pictures away. At the time they didn't mean much to me. I'd heard Mom talk about her friend Ruth. There was Janet who had beautiful red hair but had to shave it all off because she became a nun. I'm not sure how true that was, but that is what I remember.

Names and more names. How would I keep them straight? I tucked them away in the back of my mind and decided to bring them back out when the time came, if the time ever came.

Lineage, Ancestry, and Genealogy

The genealogy bug took hold of me while working on the history of the school. I'd written the letter to my father without gaining results but surely there had to be a way I could get information. Not until 1995 when I lived in Oklahoma, and with the help of a friend from work, did my digging seriously commence.

My friend, Tammy, took me to where she did her search for family members – the Latter Day Saints (LDS) church where they have extensive genealogy files. She was gracious to show me around and introduce me to Marion, the receptionist. Thus, began my trek through thousands of files.

Marion said, "First place to start is the census. This will show you where your ancestors lived, worked, and who was living within the same household."

She showed me how to order microfilm and then how to thread the film on the reader. I sat for hours squinting into the small lit screen of reel after reel of antiquated media searching for my Eisentrager family. I figured if my father wasn't going to be forthcoming with information, then I'd start from the beginning and find out who my ancestors were on my own.

Throughout the years many families moved about frequently. How lucky I was as mine stayed pretty close to one area most of their lives. With the census, I found my third great-grandfather starting out in Illinois from Germany, the date he arrived in America, then moving on to Hampton and Dumont, Iowa. I also found the date of his naturalization and got a copy of it. All of this I recorded on the forms Marion gave me. She said, "It helps to keep all your records in one place and you can see what you have. And, don't forget to put the date you found it."

My grandfather and grandmother were the first to move from Iowa to Minnesota, but they lived there until they passed away. My father also.

Marion guided me through this process – what a jewel in genealogy. If I got stuck on something, I'd bounce it off her. Her guidance was priceless. She pointed out little areas I'd overlooked. I still hear her when I'm searching for something now. "Don't forget to read everything the census says about your ancestor. Each year they add something new which gives you more insight into who your family was."

I was so eager to find out where they lived, I failed to jot down their occupations as sometimes it changed. My third great-grandfather, Nathaniel Green, went from carpenter to farmer and I missed it, only spotted it after having to go back and re-read, several times.

Marion's most important bit of information was, "Remember, you need to have the paper to back up what you've found. Birth certificates, death certificates, land papers, things that prove what you said is true, and that it belongs to your ancestor."

So, I went to Walmart and bought a zippered three-ring binder and a box of archival sleeves to keep my papers. I began to drown in paperwork, but I had backup. My binder began to bulge.

When I finally found my Eisentrager grandparents in Austin, Minnesota, I found their addresses in the city directories. From there, I had to find marriage certificates. My excitement soared over the top, I was putting together my beginning as well as finding ancestors.

Then, I hit my first brick wall. I couldn't find my parent's marriage certificate. After all, they lived in Austin, Minnesota, so they had to get married there, right? The first thing I learned about ancestry was to think outside the box. Just because that seemed plausible, that is not what happens.

Since Austin is not too far from the Iowa state line, they could have married there. For some reason, I had not figured out, and had not researched, but they did get married in Northwood, Iowa. The cost of all these certificates would be astronomical but I had to make sure I had my paperwork in place. Sometimes you can get a reduced price on a certificate when you let the clerk know you need the certificate for genealogy purposes. It doesn't hurt to ask.

One day I was sitting with Marion discussing what I'd found on my ancestors and feeling quite proud of myself. However, I still had that one question. "Why did they divorce?" It never really bothered me, but it was a logical question, and I wanted to know. I was tired of dead ends and no one offering information.

Marion pushed her chair back and casually asked. "Why don't you get their divorce papers?"

"You can get that?"

"Sure, you can. They're public records. Just call or write the court house where they got the divorce."

I thought about it for a minute. "I'm sure they divorced in Austin. That's where they lived, so it would make sense they divorced there."

"Then start there." She smiled, and I'm sure she thought to herself, *finally she is getting this ancestry thing*. "Keep me posted."

That night I sat down and wrote a

letter to the clerk at the courthouse in Austin, Minnesota. I gave all the information I knew and prayed I'd get an answer.

A week later, I received a phone call from the clerk. She asked, "Are you sure you want all the paperwork on this case?"

What was she talking about? "What do you mean all the paperwork?"

"There's over two hundred pages of the court report. At twenty-five cents a piece that could be a bit costly. Are you sure you want it all?"

"Oh, I see what you mean. What do you recommend?"

"Well, you can get the petition and the answer." She paused. "That wouldn't cost as much."

"What is that?"

"It's where the petitioner asked for the divorce and the answer is what the defendant signs for the petitioner."

"That sounds like a reasonable request. At least I'd know why he/she asked for the divorce and I'd get the answer. How much would that be?"

She told me, and I said. "I'll get the check in the mail in the morning."

Now the wait began. A week passed before the envelope arrived. My husband and I had finished our day at work and arrived home ready to put our feet up for the evening. In my shaking hand I held the large manila jacket. Butterflies fluttered in my stomach. What would I find out once I opened the pouch? I sat down on the stool at the counter and slowly lifted the flap, removed the papers, and began reading.

"Oh, my goodness. Oh, my goodness." I stood up. I sat down. "Oh, my goodness."

My husband walked by but didn't say a word. He stopped and watched me read.

I saw it as plain as day. *Petitioner, Roy Eisentrager, requests divorce on grounds of infidelity while he was out of the country during World War II. Annabell Eisentrager had an affair with one, Bud Wyburn, and from this union a child was born* – with my birthdate recorded. "Oh, my goodness."

My husband said, "What is it?"

"Here." I handed him the papers. "You read it."

He began. "I'm so sorry."

"Thank you. It wasn't your fault; you weren't there."

"No, but I'm sorry you had to find it out this way."

My brain began rationalizing what I had just read. Maybe Mom signed the paperwork because she skimmed over it, didn't really read everything carefully, and she was embarrassed. Was there more to the story than what was in the papers? Nothing made sense.

Too stunned to breathe, too shocked to cry. Never in all my years could I have thought this scenario happened. My life had been a lie all along. I thought about how my stepfather, Harold, who brought me up, dried my tears, listened to my complaints, and he wasn't my biological father. Now seeing this, Roy wasn't my father either. Who was this Bud person? Where did he come from? Where did he live? How did they meet? I had more questions than answers, and I felt my head spinning. I thought *just wait till I tell Marion. She'll tell me where to go from here.*

Legacy, Heredity, Bloodline

All the work I'd accomplished for the past year, yes, it took me a year to find what information I had on the Eisentrager lineage. My binder was filled with scrapbooked pictures, people I'd met during this time, all for naught. Or was it?

I met cousins of the Eisentragers, and we spent Thanksgiving with them one year. We remained friends until their passing. They were quite a bit older than me. The cousins were the ones who gave me pictures of the family, and for that I am thankful and indebted.

Through it all, I did find out I am related to the Eisentragers, like fourth cousins. My maternal grandmother Bessie Valentine, was the cousin of Sieby Diekman Eisentrager. Both are descendants of Ausbrand Valentine. Whew, confusing!

If I hadn't gone through all that, I wouldn't have found the last piece of evidence of my parents' lives. Now on to my next endeavor. Another binder to buy and fill.

Okay, pen and paper ready, let's see who Bud Wyburn was. Where was he from? I turned the computer on and started looking for where all the Wyburns lived. I tried white pages, yellow pages, and googled where do Wyburns live. I wanted to look closely to people living in and around the tri-state area. Since we lived in Minnesota, I thought he had to be from Iowa, Wisconsin, or maybe even Illinois. I wrote down addresses and names. The letter writing began.

I didn't want to scare anyone off by telling them I was looking for my father. Who would want to open a letter and start reading that? What kind of trouble could that cause between family members? To be fair, because maybe in the back of my mind I still wasn't sure, I started my letter by saying I was looking for Bud Wyburn because he was a friend to my parents during the forties and I had found pictures I thought he might like to have. I had pictures, but I wasn't sure who was who in them. It was worth a shot.

One letter I received said she didn't know anything about the Wyburn line, but she gave me the name of a lady in Wisconsin, along with her address, who was doing research on that line. It was worth the letter, envelope, and stamp to see what she could tell me. More waiting.

While waiting for an answer, I went to the church, talked to Marion, and began the process all over again. I ordered census films for Wisconsin and Iowa and began filling out my forms again. I wasn't able to find anyone by the name of "Bud," but I already figured that had to be a nickname. The big job ahead of me was trying to figure out his first name, plus, figure out his age.

I sat down and gave his age a shot. Mom was born in 1924. My step-father was born in 1919. Roy Eisentrager was born in 1919. Would she date anyone younger than her? I didn't think so. I could be wrong, but I was going for older like 1916 through 1919. I felt safe with that.

The Stranger in the Polka Dot Tie

I took my bulletin board and pinned sticky notes all over it (pinned because the sticky notes kept falling off). First came his name, then his approximate date of birth, and last the state he may have lived in. More letter writing because I hadn't received answers from the first batch of questions I'd sent out.

While waiting for someone to answer, I went back to Mom's photo albums and looked at the pictures again. What was I missing? Most of the pictures were small, and I couldn't make out details. I made a note of where they were in the album and took them to Walgreens to enlarge to a 4 X 6. All of the ones I took were of Junior Waverly. For some reason, this person intrigued me. Having them enlarged made it easier to see details, but I was still in the dark, so to speak, on who he was and why Mom kept them. Junior was a good looking, fair haired person with a thin David Niven type mustache. I took the picture of him in his uniform and pinned it to the bulletin board, then put the rest in a box.

While waiting for answers, I decided to try to find this Junior. After all, my mother seemed to be pretty friendly with him. How did he fit into the scheme of things? Again, I began with the census for Minnesota. Nothing. On to Iowa. Nothing. Who is this guy? I laid it aside.

Finally, a letter from the lady in Wisconsin with all the information she had on Alfred Wyburn. She was searching for clues for his maternal side of the genealogy, not the paternal. By this time, I'd received another letter from the Wyburn side from a different town in Wisconsin. She shared with me the paternal side of the family.

We quickly became genealogy friends. (Judy searching the maternal side of family). Letters flew back and forth. Then Judy sent me a picture of young Alfred sitting with his mother and grandmother. When I looked at his picture, I immediately thought of a picture I had at the same age and how similar they were. I made a copy and mailed it back, along with a copy of the one she sent me, hoping she saw the same resemblance. She said she did, thus began our journey together of researching the Wyburn family. We both were convinced we had found my father. Only he was killed in an electrical accident in the fifties.

By this time, I had been working on my genealogy for five years. I started earnestly in 1995, right after my mother passed away. It was now 2000, and I felt like I hadn't gotten very far.

My binder was growing with birth certificates, death certificates, and copies of the census reports. My father lived in and around Dubuque, Iowa, all his life, never venturing very far. When I found the date of his joining the Army, I was able to figure out a timeline for him as to where he was stationed. Something wasn't matching though. I kept trying to tie him to Austin; Judy took a stab at it. I had to see if he had traveled to Minnesota to visit relatives and maybe that was when he met my mother. Judy tried to think of what relative lived in Austin. We were not having much luck.

I laid it aside as Judy gave me information of Alfred's second great-grandmother, Katie, who was a full blood Sac Indian who survived the Black Hawk War in 1832. Oh, now I was intrigued over this. The more I read about her, the more I wanted to tell her story. For the next five years, I wrote Katie's story and looked for more information on Alfred.

During lulls in writing and researching, I went back to look for Junior Waverly. This guy was a ghost. There was no Junior Waverly on the face of the earth that lived close to Austin, Minnesota. I knew Junior had to be a nickname. Another genealogy friend said, "Perhaps Waverly is the first name."

On and on it went like that until 2007, the year I took my first DNA test with Family Tree DNA. The door opened.

We'd moved back to Texas in 2001 because of my husband's job. We bought a house, and I began enjoying my grandchildren living closer to us. The rest of our children were scattered across the states, so it was nice to be close to one of the girls. One of our daughters was in the Air Force, so she was stationed one place then another. One son served in the Marines and his life was somewhat the same. Another son was my desert hermit. He enjoyed his life living along the Colorado River in Arizona. Two of my daughters lived in Washington state, quite spread out.

Everyone was talking about DNA. The most popular seemed to be Family Tree DNA. When I looked at the prices, I thought no way, I can't afford that. But the seed was planted. I had told a friend several years earlier, "If only there was DNA, then I'd find out who my father was."

Frustration always looked me in the face. I just couldn't put the pieces of the puzzle together to come up with a picture. By this time, I was using Ancestry to gather all my information.

Occasionally I used Google and typed in the county and state of where I was searching for clues, then I'd type in genealogy and history. Sometimes their historical society had a wonderful website with more material than Ancestry. If I found the data I was looking for, I'd send them an e-mail and ask for the copy they had. They, in turn, told me how much it cost for the copy, then they e-mailed it to me once I paid. I received my third great-grandfather Green's land papers by this procedure. It has helped me on numerous other occasions too.

About the umpteenth time I visited the Family Tree DNA website, I stopped and prayed. "All right, Lord, if this is what I'm supposed to do, give me peace about it." I did it, asked for my kit, and paid the price. Yes, I did have peace, even at the price I paid.

Now the wait began. When I received my kit, I immediately took the sample and mailed it off. Another wait...

Within eight weeks, I received an e-mail saying I could go to the website and get my results. There, I found charts, maps, numbers, letters, and, oh, so mind boggling. I had an "A" this and a "T" that. It listed my autosomal numbers and right away, I had matches. Names with sequences and centimorgans. I didn't understand anything. Nothing. *(See Appendix Figure 1: Autosomal)*

Well, if I couldn't figure out any of this stuff, I thought I'd just buy a book on DNA and that would help me. How hard could that be? I bought *Trace Your Roots with DNA Using Genetic Tests to Explore Your Family Tree* by Megan Smolenyak Smolenyak and Ann Turner. After all, Megan is an authority on this kind of thing.

However, after reading it, I was even more confused. I made copies of my ethnicity and the maps and put them all nice and neat into a three-ring binder. Then I could go back to the website and maybe figure out things.

And, so I did. And, no, I still couldn't figure out anything. First of all, the matches I found had names I'd never heard of. Mind you, I'm still looking for names like Eisentrager, Waverly, and Wyburn. This was turning into more of a challenge than I'd bargained for. How was I ever going to pinpoint that one person in my life?

This went on for months and months before I gave up. There had to be another way. Then the Schertz Genealogical Society announced a meeting and the guest speaker was a man who knew DNA inside out. That was how he found his family members. This was going to be a meeting I wasn't going to miss.

The night of the meeting I sat intently watching his diagram on DNA and how he was able to find so many people in his lineage. I had to get a few minutes with him for a one on one. Usually, I would quietly exit and go about my way but not tonight. I edged my way right up beside him and barged in the first chance I got. "Can you tell me what I'm doing wrong? I had my DNA done by Family Tree DNA, but I can't figure it out."

"Let's go into the genealogy room and use the computer so I can see what you're talking about. Do you remember your login?"

"Yes, I do."

After logging in, he scanned each page. "You just had the mtDNA done. Did you know that?"

"What is the mtDNA? I didn't know there was a difference."

"Oh, yes, there is a difference. mtDNA is your mother's line. In other words, you are getting matches from your maternal side of DNA. You need a male to show your paternal side and only males can have the "Y" DNA done." *(See Appendix Figure 2: Chromosome Browser)*

"Well, that's not going to happen. I don't know who my father is. That's why I took the DNA test, to find out who my biological father is. Now what do I do?"

"I suggest having more markers done.

Like the autosomal and it gives you more information. I would also suggest taking the Family Finder test. It will put you in touch with anyone in the whole family line."

"What do you mean by that?"

He took out a piece of paper and drew a picture of me, then my parents. I do better with pictures. "Say someone in, maybe a fifth cousin on your paternal side, has his DNA done. He comes up as one of your matches. There is your first clue."

"But I don't have a name to begin with."

"Then you will probably have to wait until you get closer matches, perhaps second or third cousins. Here's my card, would you keep me posted on your progress?"

"I can do that. Thank you for explaining this for me. It makes a bit more sense."

It made sense, but after looking at it, all I could think about was spending more money. Money I wasn't prepared to spend. Still...

The more I thought about it, the more passionate I became about finding my father. Mr. "C" (my husband) was earning good wages right now so I took the plunge. I signed up for the Family Finder at Family Tree DNA. They already had my DNA, all they had to do was another test. Then I signed up for two more tests on the autosomal, more markers. From all this, surely, I was going to find something new.

I went back to the book I'd purchased and started reading, again. There are two lines, the Y chromosome and the MtDNA. This is only a tiny fraction of one's total ancestry. Every little snippet of your DNA comes from one of your ancestors, but which one? That's what I'm saying, "Which one?" I closed the book.

While waiting for results, I continued to work on my book about Katie, the Sac Indian girl. Even though she wasn't my third great-grandmother, by now, I was so interested in her story, I wanted to tell it. I wanted to be her voice. There was so much written about her in the history of Wisconsin, Illinois, and Iowa, but I wanted to give her story a human touch. She was a woman, a wife, mother, but more important, she was a pioneer in her own right. Katie was only one out of thousands of women who survived massacres, plagues, childbirth, and the ravages of everyday life during the early

1800's. This sounds crazy, but I felt a oneness with Katie; she was personal.

So, now, back to DNA. Through Family Finder, I received matches. Again, everything from fourth to eighth matches with names I'd never heard of. More markers, more frustrations. With Family Finder I did have a second cousin match. She listed the names she was researching, and I found two names which matched who I was searching. After figuring out how we were related, we met in Clyde, Texas, and spent the afternoon together. She gave my husband and me the tour of their land, homes, and even the new cemetery her father had just finished for their final resting place. What a lovely day spent with another one of my maternal side of the family. Not the side I was looking for, but now she is not only a cousin, but we consider each other friends. We still keep in touch. More information to store in the family tree book. My book of life, the year is now 2011.

Each day I checked my DNA with Family Tree. Nothing. Ancestry was now doing DNA with a reduced price. I took the plunge again.

First, they lost my sample. Second one they couldn't find... I took my numbers from Family Tree and entered it with Ancestry. Now to wait for matches. I got the same thing, all fourth to eighth cousins on both sites. I tried once to see if I could at least find one name and figure out how we were related. It was mind boggling, too many names, too far out there, so I gave up. I needed a closer counterpart.

I worked on Katie, my book. I checked my matches, I researched family members of who I already knew of. More information to put in my zippered binders. They were growing leaps and bounds. It was a good thing the binder had a fastener, because I began shoving the information in and closing it up instead of placing it in archival sleeves. Newspaper articles, city directories, and family stories people put on line gave me an inside look as they found their family members.

Ancestry started putting my matches up and they, too, were from fourth to eighth. Way out there. One day while talking with my half-brother, Chuck, I told him how frustrated I was getting because I was getting nowhere.

How was I ever going to figure out this mess? He had been doing his father's side of ancestry himself. He and his wife even took a trip to Sweden to meet cousins he'd found while researching.

While discussing this with him, he asked me, "Do you think Mom would have ever told you who your father was?"

I thought for a second while remembering my conversations with Mom. "Yes, I think she would have – if I'd asked the right question. I never asked the right question."

"What do you mean by that?"

"Every time I'd ask her about my father, she was talking about Eisentrager. That's because she always told me he was my father. Now that I know he wasn't, I would have rephrased my questions."

"You may be right."

"I picture the scenario with mom like this. After asking her about my biological father she would start crying because she was embarrassed. Maybe because she had been caught in a lie, who knows. In the end, I think after all the crying, she would have come clean.

We will never know."

"Yeah, it's probably better she took it to her grave."

My brother had his DNA done with Ancestry to help me out and his name came up on my matches as a close match, family member, or sibling. I then went to his site and I was able to see if we had matching people. If we did, I'd put a star by the name and that way I'd know I didn't have to check all the names Ancestry had listed. I went to the next match and tried to figure out how we were related.

Again, though, most of my matches were third, fourth to eighth. Way out there. Then one day in 2014, I found a second cousin that was a match. He had a lot of names listed, none that I recognized, but then, I didn't have a name to begin with. This was going to be a challenge.

Forms, White Board, Papers and More Papers.

R.B. (he used his initials and not his name) compiled a wonderful array of names, dates, and places. But, again, which name was I looking for? I started with the first name he recorded, took my forms from American Ancestors, and wrote the names.

First, I filled out the parents' names, DOB and where they were born, DOD and where they died. If he had a date of marriage, I listed it also, and if there were children, I inscribed them. *(See Appendix Figures 3 and 4: Family Group Sheets)*

Then I'd go to Ancestry and find where they were living in the census. Since there isn't a place to jot down census, city directories, etc., I turned the paper over and entered the date of the census, where they lived, worked, everything I could find about the person. This way every little thing I found was all on one piece of paper, nothing to get lost.

The important thing was to find people who lived in Iowa, Wisconsin, Minnesota, or Illinois. If they didn't live in those states, I'd go on to the next person he had itemized. Those were the people I did more research on. A long process and a lot of paperwork. Time consuming but this is what worked for me. I saw what was before me in writing, and I could clip together the names that didn't work and keep the others out in case I had to refer back to them.

I used a bulletin board in the beginning, but I after watching a lot of Forensic Files and homicide shows on television, I realized they used a white board to put all their information about the cases they were working on. I liked the concept. I bought a white board.

By the time I got to the third name R.B. had listed, I had a stack of paper. Too much paper. Another idea came to mind – I hadn't used the Search Matches button before with my matches. I didn't know how it worked, but I determined to figure it out. Maybe it would help me narrow down my search.

At the top of the page on the right-hand side is an oblong block, "Search Matches." When you hit that, it slides over and you can type a last name in it and all of your matches who are searching the same name will come up. I struck pay dirt.

I typed in "Mattocks," and all my matches with the same last name came up. Why hadn't I'd seen this before. Guess I had blinders on. I took R.B.'s name and wrote it on my white board and wrote second cousin. I did the same for every corresponding name. He was the closest; the rest were fourth cousins.

I was in luck as each person who had the name "Mattocks" listed with the same first names had one or two different dates and places. Time to really do some digging.

Daniel married Elizabeth Hays/Hayes then added their children starting with Cordellia, as the same name my other counterparts also listed in their ancestry. They were living in Pennsylvania but eventually moved to Iowa. Now we were cooking. I started out with the year of Daniel's birth – 1806. Stacks of paper started to mound up!

I reasoned I was looking for a male, born between 1915 to 1920 and had to be living in or around Austin, Minnesota. My mother was born in 1924, so he had to be a bit older than her. After all, my stepfather was born in 1919; Eisentrager, her first husband was born in 1918, so the man I was looking for should be around that age too. As I said, this was my thought, and I worked with it.

When I added names to my Family Group

Sheet, from American Ancestors, I also attached a small sticky note to each of the children who were matches to me on my Ancestry DNA. With the white board and this, I could keep each child separated.

    I started with the first child, Cordellia. I took the information on her, then added another third cousin's data, and attached the statistics I found from Family Search and Ancestry. I had so much paper by now I could wallpaper my office. The only problem was nothing jived with anything I could use. There had to be a better way but finding that way was beginning to be a challenge.

    I went back to the first set of papers I started, Daniel and Elizabeth. The next child was Permelia, in line with R.B. my second cousin. She married Burton Kinsel, and I listed all their children. If I found out who they married I added their names too. More paperwork.

    I wasn't getting anywhere so I went on to the next child, and the next repeating the process with each one. Almost every child of Daniel and Elizabeth had at least five to seven children. As you can see, the paper trail magnified. When I could no longer see straight, I'd stop, kick back in my chair and stare at the computer. My head reeled with names, dates, and places. So many questions floated around and around in my mind.

Life goes on; I had a story to finish and I wanted to get it out there for people to read. I felt a bond, a kinship if you will, with Katie, Indian Kate. She had my heart. She was just as real while I wrote about her as when she lived. I guess when I thought she was my third great-grandmother, I fell in love with her and her story. Anyway, I plugged away on my computer, so I could put the book to bed.

I took trips with my daughter, joined in monthly get-togethers with my girlfriends, had our weekly breakfast morning with the girls, and yes, kept house for the love of my life Mr. 'C'. Mr. 'C' is my first priority. He says I'm a contemporary "Miss Marple."

The Thursday morning breakfast gals heard about my frustrations almost weekly and they were most kind. One of the ladies is also a genealogist and she helped me try to figure out who Junior Waverly was. For some reason, I kept coming back to his picture.

February 16, 2016, *White Moccasins, the Story of Katie* was released. Book signings began. But I was still pounding away at the computer working on my Mattocks line. Everyone I found in that line lived in and around Waterloo, Iowa. Right area, but for some reason, no names surfaced.

One morning I pulled out the paperwork on Daniel and Elizabeth again. I zeroed in on Permelia who married James Kinsel. This was R.B.'s line and R.B. was my closest cousin. There had to be someone I was missing. Again, I looked over each child's name and who they married. So maybe the surname I was looking for was Kinsel. I sat back in my chair and scanned the whiteboard again. Each one of the cousins who had Mattocks also listed Kinsel.

Out came the American Ancestor forms again, and I took the first Kinsel R.B. listed and placed it on the first line. His birthdate, place of birth, date of death, place of death, and who he married. If there was a date of marriage, I entered it. Next, I jotted down her name with date of birth, place, and so on. The same procedure as I did with the Mattocks line.

The census came next by turning the forms over and inscribing the date of the census, where it was taken, date it was taken, then each person living in the home at the time. I also noted what page it was on from Ancestry. It would be like: 1880 Census, IA, Black Hawk, Waterloo, (page 4 Ancestry). This shows where I found the information. I documented where I found the data, so I could return to look at it later if need be. It also lets others know where you found the material, so they can look it up if so inclined.

It sounds crazy, I was on a roll but, alas, paper mounted up again and I was getting nowhere. I was still looking for a male born between 1915 and 1920 and he had to have lived in Iowa, Minnesota, or Wisconsin.

Most of the time, I searched Ancestry for my closest relatives. Virtually all were fourth, fifth, and up to eighth kinsmen. One day after much vexation, I logged out of Ancestry and went to Family Tree DNA to see if I had any new counterparts. Much to my surprise, my brother was at the top of my listings. He must have had his DNA analyzed to help me out like he did on Ancestry. I love that boy!

Since I was on the website, I looked at each name once again. Lo and behold, I had a new name and he listed some of the names he was researching. There was Kinsel and he had his genealogy listed also. I placed the information on my forms, logged out of the site and went back to Ancestry. Went through the process once again, and once more nothing, close but nothing.

Another day to begin the same things I'd been doing for the past twenty years all over. Take care of the house, take care of the dogs, then sit down to the computer. You'd think I would have tired of the computer, but by now my passion for discovering who my father was had a tight grip on me. Every waking moment I thought of him and, *where was he?* Was he still alive and what was he doing? I felt like I was getting close but yet so far away. One more time, one more name to look up.

I was still trying to figure out who Junior Waverly was. The name of Waverly seemed to be a favorite first name for men during the 30's and 40's so I even tried to figure out if one of them was the man I was looking for. Nothing ever came of it. Either they lived too far away, or they stayed right where they were born and raised.

Since I couldn't make heads or tails of Waverly and nothing jelled on Ancestry or Family Tree DNA, I decided to look on 23andme.com. I'd held off having my DNA tested with them because I thought between the two sites, I'd find who I was looking for with no problem. Well now was the time to try this website. My test had been sent in for some time so now was the time to see if I had any relatives.

I typed www.23andme.com, logged in and went to Tools then DNA relatives. The name of Kinsel appeared and he was a second cousin. That was really close. Out came the forms again, and I began the process. I had it whittled down to one person, Clarence Kinsel, but he didn't have any boys. Right place in Iowa though. I was missing something. What?

Clarence was listed in the 1930 census with a wife and a daughter. I looked in the 1920 census, and he was listed with another wife and a son. Oh, my goodness, that son was born in 1918. I went back to the 1930 census looking for the wife and son. Nothing. What was I doing wrong? I sat and stared at the computer. Maybe the wife and son were killed in a car wreck. I couldn't find any information on either one. I tried pulling up death certificates, nothing. They had to be somewhere.

After sitting for a while, I got up and let the dogs out, then gave them a treat. I took a break, got a cookie and a diet coke, and went back to the computer. I will find them this time!

I pulled up Ancestry then typed the mother's first and last name. Nothing. I went back to the 1920 census and calculated her date of birth and his too. Both were born in Iowa. Then I went back and typed in his name with a date of birth. Nothing. Okay, I would approach it another way. I typed in her first name and living in Iowa with her date of birth. There it was. She had divorced and remarried. I made a copy of the information. More paper trail. This time I went to the 1930 census and typed her new husband's name in with his date of birth and state. The whole family appeared along with the Kinsel son with the date of birth of 1918. He was going by his stepfather's last name, not his birth name. I heaved a sigh of relief and let the tears flow. I knew I had him. I just knew it.

My mind started wandering . . . what a coincidence between the two of us. My stepfather never adopted me, but I always used his last name. Now this man was using his stepfather's last name too. I tried looking for some kind of document telling me he had been adopted but found nothing.

Oh, what a doubting Thomas I was. I felt like I took one step forward, then I'd doubt myself and my findings, and take two steps backward. More investigating needed to be done. Was this really the man I was looking for? Why couldn't I find any more information on him? I found where he married and stayed in one place all his life. Surely, he went to Minnesota and met my mother. One answer produced another question.

I just needed to figure out if he did

go north or he stayed in Iowa all the time. I decided to follow up on Wesley's stepfather's relatives. Maybe the connection was there.

It seemed like the puzzle pieces began to fit. His stepfather had quite a few cousins, aunts, and uncles living in Iowa but now it was time to see if there were some in Austin, Minnesota. Out came city directories, census and anything else I could find to pinpoint where people were at a certain time. My favorite word "Bingo." I found it.

Wesley did have relatives living in Austin. There it was. At some point in time, he had to have met my mother, or rather, I wanted to believe this theory. It had to be it.

I still hadn't found the relative who Wesley went to visit in Austin, but at some point, either they knew my mother, or both mom and Wesley just happened to bump into each other. That could be another story there.

Putting All the Puzzle Pieces Together

I couldn't wait to tell my girlfriends at my weekly breakfast. My genealogy friend, Rushelle, jumped at a chance to help me find more information. I gave her what I'd found; she went home and began her search.

Between the two of us, we were able to dig deep enough and find Wesley's wife and children's names. Everything was coming together all at one time. My book, *White Moccasins* was finished and ready to be printed. To say my excitement was over the top was an understatement. Between these two events, I was giddy. I wanted to laugh and cry at the same time.

Rushelle found my sister's names plus my stepmother's name and dates. However, we could not locate my father, Wesley, after 1944. We didn't think too much of it as Ancestry had brought dates up to 1940 and some up to 1944 on their web site, but not everything was listed. Meanwhile, Ancestry kept adding more and more each day to help people find their ancestors' lives.

Cibolo Coffee Haus, where I go to write each week, sponsored a book signing for me, so here was another thing I had going. My granddaughter is on the cover of my book, so she was there for the signing too. She now tells everyone she is famous.

With all of this going on I was still able to find some more information about my father's family. Social media is good and sometimes not so good. I was pleased to find a sister-in-law on Facebook living in Waterloo, Iowa. Since I was going to meet my cousin in Wisconsin, I thought it might work out going through Waterloo and meeting a brother. It was worth a shot. I messaged her and explained what I'd found and asked her if maybe we could get together. Then I prayed. After all, I'd gotten this far, I had to continue.

My cousin in Wisconsin ordered two boxes of books to deliver to relatives of Katie

(*White Moccasins*) and give to libraries in the area. If it hadn't been for Judy giving me all the information on Katie there wouldn't have been a book. And at one point, when Judy and I thought we were related through DNA, I thought Katie was my great great-grandmother too. But Judy and I still call each other cousins anyway.

    I continued looking for more information on the internet. In the meantime, I did find a third cousin who had put together a very lengthy family tree and he invited me to his site to get any information I needed. I will forever be indebted to him as it helped me immensely. It really helps when you have people helping each other instead of keeping their finds to themselves. Thank you, Perry.

    As the time came closer for our trip to Wisconsin, I decided to ask Judy if she would mind driving over to Waterloo to pick up the boxes of books. I called her and said, "Maybe I could set up a time to meet my new-found brother, give him a book, and find out some more information. That is, if he is willing to meet me."

"No problem," she said. "It's not that far of a drive. Sure. When?"

All my information started coming in fast and furious. I found a half-sister living in Missouri, so I wrote her a letter. I asked if we could meet. In the past, when writing a letter asking about an individual I was looking for, I'd tell them I was looking for a friend of my parents, and that I'd found pictures in my mother's albums along with their names. I told them I'd like to pass the pictures along to them. My purpose was not to turn the individual off, scare them or have them think I wanted anything from them.

But, writing this letter had a mind of its own. I couldn't help myself. I spilled my guts. In a frenzy, my pen got way ahead of me. I explained who I was, that my husband and I would be going to Missouri for Veteran's week, why I'd like to meet with her, and asked if she would be willing to meet with me. Before I mailed the letter, I grabbed the pictures of my mother with Junior Waverly, made copies, and asked her if she might know who this man was. Maybe she did, what would it hurt to throw it in the envelope too?

I hesitated before sealing the envelope. I rationalized that if I'd gotten a letter from someone telling me they were my relative, I'd probably be a bit skeptical. I don't know if I'd answer the letter or throw it in the trash. You never know what you would do in a situation like that. So, I did the next best thing. I dismissed it. The last thing I wanted to do was force myself on anyone. I knew what I'd found, and I was okay with that.

Puzzle Completed

The week came. I loaded two cases of my *Katie* books in the back of our suburban, and hubby and I headed to Iowa. In working with genealogy, I had found two cousins on my mother's paternal side of the family, one in Des Moines, and the other in Omaha, Nebraska. We had talked back and forth so I'd decided to meet with them along the way. Hopefully, we'd find a restaurant along IH 35 and have lunch together. Of course, that depended on what time we made it close to the destination. Long story short, we were not able to make the connection, but I'm sure there will be another time.

As we drove east on Highway 20, I watched the vast rolling hills of newly planted crops go by. Then I spotted a small church and cemetery. "Look that's the cemetery we visited on our trip a few years ago," I said to hubby. "My grandparents are buried there, or rather the ones I thought were my grandparents. I know where we are now. Parkersburg is just up the road." The realization hit me like a slap upside the head. We had been there back in 1997 at Thanksgiving when we visited with the relatives who I thought were my cousins.

"I recognize the church too," my husband said. "Look, there's a sign. Waterloo is just down the road."

"I never realized these towns were so close together. My mother's mother had to have gone to Waterloo at some time or another. She may have run into family members, or maybe even known some of them." Cold chills ran down my back. Everyone was so close to each other.

Upon entering the city limits of Waterloo, I tried to take in every detail of the town. My father was born, died, and was buried there. Everything was happening so fast. I wanted to slow down and savor each minute. Let it all sink in slowly.

Our hotel sat on a main thoroughfare

close to quite a few familiar restaurants and a Walmart. You know you've arrived in any town when you spot a Walmart. It would be handy if we needed any supplies. It was late in the afternoon, so we checked in and emptied the Suburban of our luggage. I wanted to get down to business, but I knew I had to go slow. The most important thing on my mind was not to scare off my new brother. I'm sure he was feeling quite anxious over meeting me, if indeed he was going to meet me. We headed to Red Lobster for dinner, since I had a gift card there. When paying for our meal, I discovered my gift card had only a dollar and a few cents on it. Note to self, make sure to keep receipt showing how much I still have on a card.

  Even though we hadn't met in person yet, my new sister-in-law and I had become friends on Facebook. I waited until the next morning to let her know we had arrived and to see when it would be a good time to meet. That is, if they still would like to meet me. I waited, almost holding my breath, for an answer. What if they didn't want to meet me? What would I do then? How would I handle being rejected? I'd come so far. All these questions circled in my mind and I am sure now that there were probably a few more. So many only I've forgotten them.

To get my mind off our meeting we decided to take a ride through town and the outlying areas. I'd already told my husband I wanted to see the Little Brown Church in Nashua. My grandmother had a brochure about it. I felt drawn to the church. Could my mother and grandmother have stopped there for some reason? After looking at the map, I found the highway from Waterloo to Austin, Minnesota, went right by the church. Back in the 1940s they must have taken this road. Plus, the Cedar River that flowed through Austin flowed right through Waterloo, too. I pointed out so many ties to both these places. Or was I wanting to find similarities?

My sister-in-law must have been looking at Facebook, because she answered my message quickly saying they would like to meet me. I messaged back to see if they could meet at our hotel around one in the afternoon. This would ensure our meeting place was neutral and no one would be intimated. At least I hoped it would put them at ease. She said that would work for them, too.

We hurried back to the hotel so I could get my paperwork together. I had thrown all the pictures of Mom and Junior in, just in case. You never know. I picked up my computer so I could show them how I calculated the DNA with my other matches. Then I paced the floor until we headed for the lobby to wait.

I searched each face that entered the hotel. Then promptly at one, they walked through the door. I immediately recognized my sister-in-law from her picture on Facebook. I stood up and waited for them to approach, introduced ourselves, shook hands, and sat down.

How should I begin? My computer was warmed up and ready to go with Ancestry. I pulled out my paperwork and laid it on the table. I do have a problem with jumping ahead — rambling, so I had to keep reminding myself to slow down. Just because I knew what I was talking about, my new-found brother, Charlie, probably didn't know anything about DNA. It was up to me to try to make it as plain as I could for him and his wife.

I watched his face and could tell he was skeptical, as he should be. Who was this woman who just walked into his life and upset the apple cart? Why was she claiming she was my sister after all these years?

We talked for a few minutes as I explained how I figured everything out through the DNA. Then to my surprise, Charlie pulled out the letter I sent to my sister in Missouri. Now I was puzzled. He said when she got the letter, she called him and told him about it, then sent everything to him. *So, he knew who I was before I even showed up.* Only he didn't know everything. I was there to put the icing on the cake.

Charlie said he tried to wrap his mind around all the information I put in the letter, but he couldn't. He shook his head when I told him I'd taken the DNA tests with Ancestry, Family Tree, and 23andMe, and found matches through all three.

I know it must have been difficult for him to understand all this new information. It took me quite a few years to even figure out what I was doing. I had tried to find people who could explain the DNA, but it was all so new there wasn't anyone who could help me. I read books, deciphered markers, and anything else I could imagine to do to determine what I was looking at. All I knew was that I had finally found who I was looking for. As I sat there talking to him, I knew in my heart, I had the right family. I felt it in my entire being.

Then, I pulled the pictures out that I'd

brought with me, slowly laying them out on the table. Charlie scrutinized each one. Then he'd look at Debbie and back to the pictures. I laid the one out that showed Junior standing by a car holding a small girl along with another man and two women next to him. Charlie recognized the man at once. "That's my Uncle David."

Then he recognized both women. He looked back at Junior. "That's my dad." He slid the picture over to Debbie. She nodded in agreement. "But I don't know whose car that is."

That was my deciding factor. That was it. Tears welled up in my eyes and flowed freely. I couldn't help it. I'd carried those pictures for twenty years. Searched and searched for Junior Waverly in every state in the union to no avail, and that was not his real name. *Mom, you hid this man so well!*

Charlie kept shaking his head as if to

clear it. How could I have pictures of his father and uncle?

"Charlie, would you like to have these pictures? I have plenty of copies."

Then came the real shocker. Charlie started speaking, almost whispering at first. "I remember hearing stories that our father did some time in jail. We were all young, so we didn't know how much were stories or facts."

He leaned back in his chair and continued. "I don't know the specifics, but it had to do with stealing a car and taking an underaged girl over the state line. Mom divorced Dad, but I don't know if they ever remarried or not. I'm fairly sure they did, as I don't believe my mother would live in sin with our father when he got out of prison."

Oh, now this was interesting. "You know, Charlie, I believe my grandmother probably had a lot to do with him going to jail. She was a very harsh woman, and from what I remember about her, I think she may have had a hand in everything that happened."

Charlie looked at me puzzled. "What do you mean?"

"I remember my mother telling me about her mother. I think she may have sent your... our dad, to jail. My mother and her father were always trying to calm her mother down as she ranted and raved over things. He usually sided with my mother and that infuriated her. Margie, Mom's sister was Grandma's favorite., She was only eight years old when she was hit by a car and killed. Mom was with her and saw it all happen." I leaned back in my chair and exhaled. "In many ways, I felt a twinge in my heart when my mother spoke about her sister and her mother. I could feel her deep hurt over not having a relationship with her mother."

Debbie covered Charlie's hand with hers. He still looked confused. I'm sure all of this information was doing an information overload, especially all at once.

"I know this is so much to take in. Just

trust me when I say, my grandmother was not an agreeable person. Mom tried and tried to smooth things over with her, no matter what the problem was. I could never figure out why Mom was forever trying to win her affection. Maybe my mother always felt unloved by her mother and wanted her approval. I don't think she ever felt like she got it. Or it may have been Mom felt responsible for Margie's death and grandma reminded her of it every chance she got."

Now, I had to know more about this. First thing I would do when I got home was to investigate this story or myth. Every family has some sort of hearsay, myth, legend. I wanted to know how much truth there was to this.

I think Charlie was eager to leave and go home to do some investigating himself. They excused themselves and stood up to leave. "Oh no, pictures first, please." I didn't come this far, or put myself out on a limb, not to at least get a picture of us together.

There was no question here. Pictures were taken, a promise to meet again before we left town, and Charlie and Debbie were on their way home. I hadn't been back to our room very long before Debbie started messaging me pictures of our father and uncle. She said Charlie was tearing through boxes of old pictures.

Debbie messaged me the next morning and said Charlie was at the court house looking for his parents' divorce and remarriage papers, which he found. A sigh of relief. We decided to meet again the next evening to talk. Just talk about our lives, our similarities, and where we went from here.

Pièce de Résistance

The next day my sister-in-law called to let me know my brother found the divorce papers from his parents plus the date of their remarriage. A sigh of relief. We met again that evening and talked for several hours. I told them we would be leaving early in the morning to head back to Texas. "I have so much more to look for to try to figure out why both of our parents went across the state line and for what reason."

Charlie said he agreed. "I'm satisfied with what I found at the court house."

"Charlie, I want you to know how blessed I am now that you've identified the man in the pictures. I've carried them for the last twenty years. I guess something inside me said hang on to them. I felt drawn to them."

Now it was my turn to investigate further.

Hugs all the way around and a promise to keep in touch.

I couldn't wait to get home. My mind was in overload trying to figure out how I was going to find the information I was looking for. Discovering who my biological father was plus meeting my half-brother should have been enough, but it wasn't. There were still questions and I wanted to find the answers.

While in Waterloo, we'd been able to locate cemeteries, graves, and the homes where the family lived at different times. Pictures were taken so I could look at them later and try to keep them in my mind. My notebook was full of short stories about other members of the family.

Once home I unpacked suitcases and was back on the computer as soon as I could. First things first. An email was sent to my friend, Collette, in Austin, Minnesota, letting her know I'd found my father and even met one brother. Collette worked in the Historical Society and steered me in the right direction on where to look for certain information. She worked closely with the Research & Archives Manager at the society, whom I'd met on my one trip to Austin. Now, I had another dilemma. How would I find if my father spent time in jail? Where should I begin? It was a long shot, but one that needed to be focused on if, indeed, he did spend time in jail in Minnesota.

I didn't have to wait long for a response. Collette told me to write to the state of Minnesota Historical Society and ask them if they have any information. Well, that made sense to me. Right away I went to www.mnhs.org and began. They have a wonderful website with so much information easily accessible and navigable. Before I knew it, I was at a site asking for information I wanted and filling out the forms. When it came to the part of payment, I hesitated for only a moment. After all, I'd come this far I had to finish. I paid $100.00 for copies, if they had anything on him. Now to wait, again. Patience and lots of it.

After about six long weeks, I received an oversized envelope from the Historical Society in Minnesota. I nervously ripped the flap open and stared at twenty-seven pages of a court report dated May 1942. I sat down. It was like reading a good fiction mystery, but it was all real. And it was my parents' story.

To get a good look at what happened let me begin with my grandfather Green's passing in December 1940 at the Veterans Hospital in Minneapolis, Minnesota. Because of the weather, they had to wait until March 1941 to bury him.

After talking with my half-brother, I think I have a better time frame of what happened. I believe my father, Wesley, went to Austin in late 1941 to visit relatives and that was when he met my mother. They struck up a friendship that led to more intimate relations. There are pictures of Wesley in my mother's albums dated 1941 but with no month. Then from other pictures dated March 1942, my mother, father, and grandmother headed west to Colorado. Also, in the pictures, were two CCC boys (unidentified), my uncle, my mother's brother, Buzzy, my half-uncle, David, with his wife, and my half-aunt, Marietta. My half-brother, Charlie, identified our uncle, wife, and aunt when I met him in Waterloo. Now here's the rest of the story.

My grandmother had placed an ad in the newspaper looking for a husband. The manuscript I received from the Historical Society stated my grandmother asked my father and mother to drive her to Sterling City, Colorado, to meet the man who had answered her advertisement.

The car was my grandmother's, so she, my mother, father (biological), and my mother's brother, Buzzy, packed the car and started out. Somewhere along the way, they picked up two CCC boys who were hitchhiking. Hitchhiking was not uncommon during this time period. My Uncle David, his wife, and my Aunt may have met with them somewhere along the way but didn't go with them to Colorado. I only know this because of pictures they were in but were not mentioned in any of the paperwork.

When they reached their destination, the man who answered my grandmother's ad said he wasn't interested in marriage. (I am only guessing here). But, Grandma and my mother's brother, Buzzy, stayed in Colorado for a few more weeks. My parents headed back to Austin, Minnesota.

The Stranger in the Polka Dot Tie

For some reason only my parents know, they did not stay in Austin, rather, they headed north to friends of theirs. When Grandma returned, her car was gone along with my parents. She filed charges against both of them saying they stole her car.

It was in May 1942 when the police finally found my parents in South Dakota. They were brought back to Austin to stand trial. The judge threw the book at my father. The first reason given was that both my mother and my father were married to other people. The second reason was that by this time, it was quite obvious my mother was pregnant. Lastly, the judge asked my father if he had his military papers. He did, and he handed them to the judge. I won't go into every detail in the paperwork but will summarize what the judge said and did.

My mother, who was eighteen at the time and married (her husband was in Europe fighting the war), was remanded to her mother's care. My father was given five years in the state reformatory in Saint Cloud, Minnesota.

My father did two years and was released. I don't know if he went to Austin to see if he could reconnect with my mother or not. From their marriage certificate, I know Wesley went back to Waterloo, Iowa, and remarried his former wife who had divorced him when he went to jail.

My mother divorced upon her husband's return from Europe. She moved to Minneapolis where she met my stepfather and married.

I'd like to say that was the end of the story, but I know there is a lot more. I'm a genealogist, and I want to know the rest of the story. I'm looking into other avenues to see if I can find the article my grandmother placed in the newspaper. My writer's mind wanders thinking of things, writing stories about these two people in love. Was it like a movie where he got out of prison and went looking for the love of his life? Or did he see the error of his ways and headed right back to the arms of a waiting wife even though she had already divorced him? I do know they remarried and went on to have more children.

I wonder if my mother wrote him letters while he was incarcerated. Did she send him pictures of me after I was born? I found a small picture of me at the age of probably two and the back said, "Love, Sandra." Could it have been a picture she sent to my father while he was in prison? Or did she write that, then not send it? She could have sent it, and it was returned to her for some reason. I will never know, but I like to let my mind wander to the "what if's" or maybe "this could have happened."

This is my story.

Stories and More Stories

In Summary

 This is my story and I've tried to put it in a simple way. However, I know it's been confusing for some to figure out. Believe me, I had to have paper and pen handy throughout the process of my search. I, too, got confused along the way.

 I belong to DNA Detectives on Facebook and read every day of individuals who have been searching for years to find their biological parents. Some have turned out good, some have not. Their stories are much like mine. My father passed away in 1973, so I never got to meet him. It would have been nice, but then again, I feel blessed to have been able to solve this puzzle. Through my half siblings, they've shown me a small part of him.

 Through it all, my Lord has taught me

patience and it wasn't in my timing, it was in His. I praise Him every day for allowing me to have closure. If you are searching for your birth parent, I pray you receive the same favor I experienced.

This has been a long search starting back in 1969 when I wrote my first letter to the Department of Military looking for an address of my father, or rather the man who I thought was my father.

In 1968, I stopped actively searching for my father when Eisentrager (who I thought was my father) answered my letter. Every now and then I'd ask my mother again about him. To which, she always said the same thing. "Oh, he was a nice man. I guess he still lives in Minnesota."

In 1995, I began searching the archives of the Mormon church in Enid, Oklahoma, reading every microfilm and microfiche I could get my hands on. I was still looking for information on Eisentrager.

In 1996 after receiving the copy of my mother's divorce papers and finding out she had an affair with Bud Wyburn, I put away all paperwork on Eisentrager. I focused my entire time looking for Wyburn. From there, I found one of his cousins in Wisconsin. By putting together everything, my new-found cousin and I were both convinced we had the right man. Oh, we were so certain. Then I took the DNA test.

Nobody came up as a match with the Wyburn name. I asked my friend in Wisconsin if she would take the test. She humored me and did it. We did not match. She was a second cousin to Wyburn, so we should have matched if I was related to him. No such luck.

In 2007, I started all over again. If I was not an Eisentrager or a Wyburn, who was I? I felt like I'd had a death in the family.

From 2008 through 2016, I worked from the computer with DNA matches. I'd had my first test done through Family Tree DNA then went to Ancestry. Not until 2015 did I finally have my DNA done through 23andMe. Between all three I was able to determine my biological father's identity.

In the end, it was DNA and the few

The Stranger in the Polka Dot Tie

pictures I had of the man in the polka dot tie that told the whole story.

Appendix

Figure 1: Ancestry Chromosome Composition

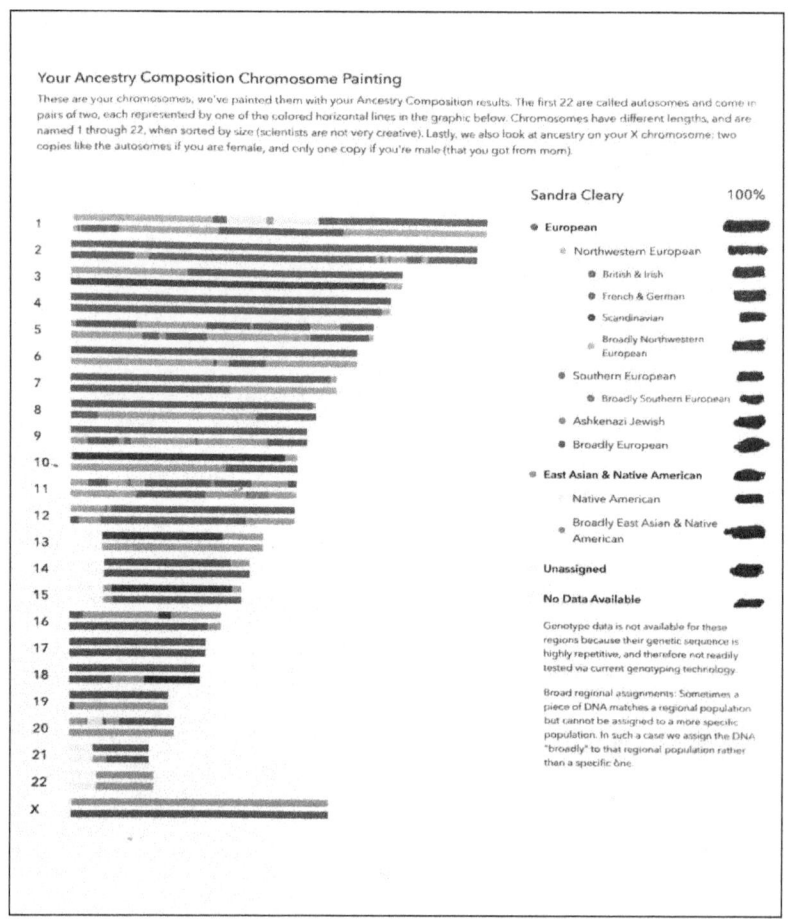

Figure 2: Autosomal Markers

Other Test Results - Autosomal Results

AUTOSOMAL CCR 5

MARKERS	VALUE
CCR5	▬▬▬▬

AUTOSOMAL MARKERS - DXYS156

MARKERS	VALUE
DXYS156	▬

AUTOSOMAL MARKERS PANEL 1

MARKERS	VALUE
CSF1PO	▬
D13S317	▬
D16S539	▬
D18S51	▬
D21S11	▬
D3S1358	▬
D5S818	▬
D7S820	▬
D8S1179	▬
FGA	▬
Penta D	▬
Penta E	▬
TH01	▬
TPOX	▬
vWA	▬

AUTOSOMAL MARKERS PANEL 2

MARKERS	VALUE
D19S433	▬
D2S1338	▬
F13A01	▬
F13B	▬
FESFPS	▬
LPL	▬

Figure 3: Family Group Sheet

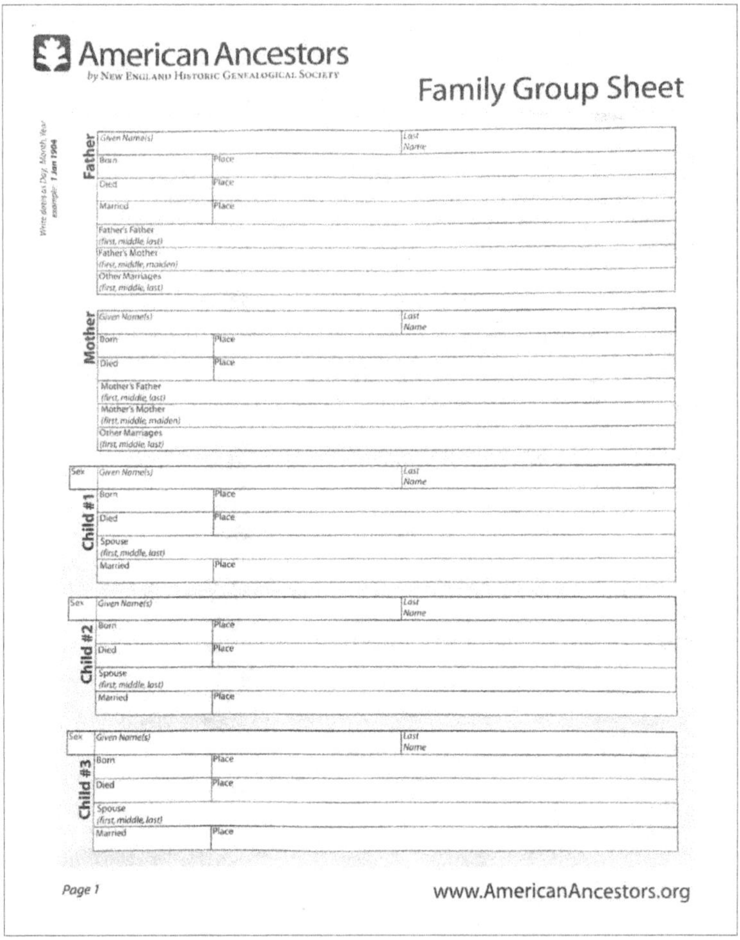

American Ancestors
by New England Historic Genealogical Society

Family Group Sheet

Write dates as Day, Month, Year
example: 1 Jan 1904

Father
Given Name(s) | Last Name
Born | Place
Died | Place
Married | Place
Father's Father (first, middle, last)
Father's Mother (first, middle, maiden)
Other Marriages (first, middle, last)

Mother
Given Name(s) | Last Name
Born | Place
Died | Place
Mother's Father (first, middle, last)
Mother's Mother (first, middle, maiden)
Other Marriages (first, middle, last)

Child #1
Sex | Given Name(s) | Last Name
Born | Place
Died | Place
Spouse (first, middle, last)
Married | Place

Child #2
Sex | Given Name(s) | Last Name
Born | Place
Died | Place
Spouse (first, middle, last)
Married | Place

Child #3
Sex | Given Name(s) | Last Name
Born | Place
Died | Place
Spouse (first, middle, last)
Married | Place

Page 1

www.AmericanAncestors.org

Figure 4: Family Group Sheet cont'd

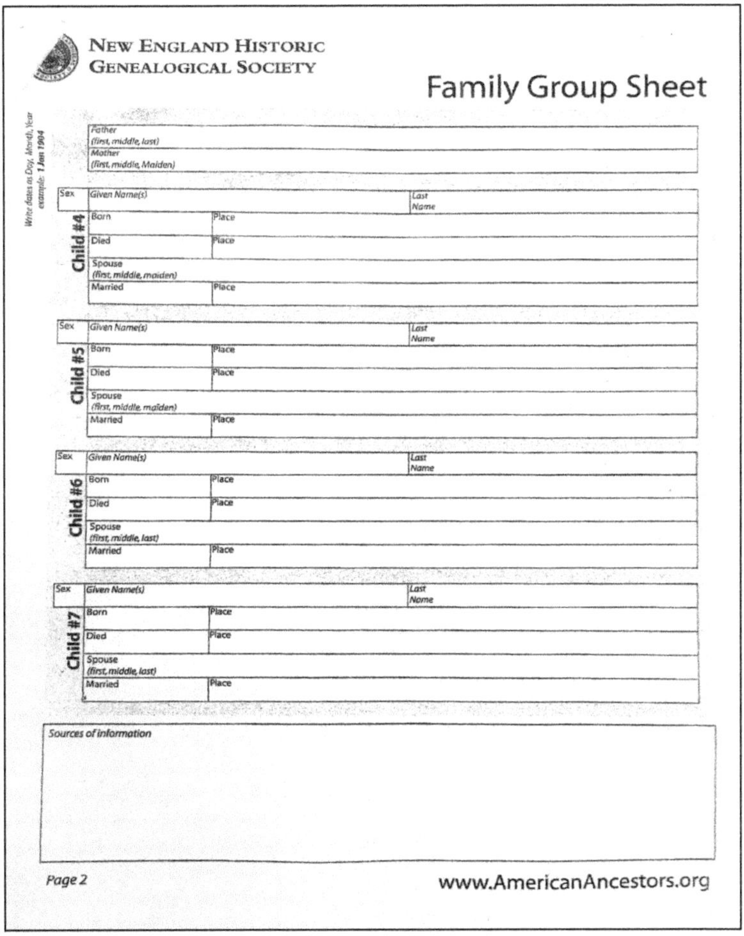
NEW ENGLAND HISTORIC GENEALOGICAL SOCIETY

Family Group Sheet

Write dates as Day, Month, Year example: 1 Jan 1904

Father (first, middle, last)			
Mother (first, middle, Maiden)			

Child #4

Sex	*Given Name(s)*		*Last Name*
	Born	Place	
	Died	Place	
	Spouse *(first, middle, maiden)*		
	Married	Place	

Child #5

Sex	*Given Name(s)*		*Last Name*
	Born	Place	
	Died	Place	
	Spouse *(first, middle, maiden)*		
	Married	Place	

Child #6

Sex	*Given Name(s)*		*Last Name*
	Born	Place	
	Died	Place	
	Spouse *(first, middle, last)*		
	Married	Place	

Child #7

Sex	*Given Name(s)*		*Last Name*
	Born	Place	
	Died	Place	
	Spouse *(first, middle, last)*		
	Married	Place	

Sources of information

Page 2 www.AmericanAncestors.org

www.ingramcontent.com/pod-product-compliance
Lightning Source LLC
Chambersburg PA
CBHW031202020426
42333CB00013B/770